NATURAL WONDERS OF THE WORLD

NILE RIVER

Erinn Banting

www.av2books.com

Step 1
Go to **www.av2books.com**

Step 2
Enter this unique code

EJZTD4JWD

Step 3
Explore your interactive eBook!

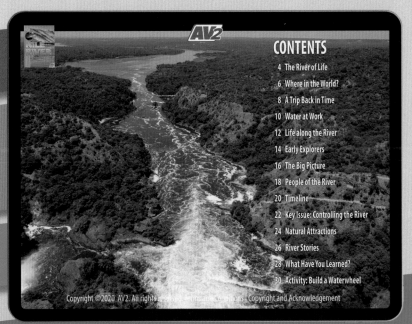

AV2 is optimized for use on any device

Your interactive eBook comes with...

Contents
Browse a live contents page to easily navigate through resources

Audio
Listen to sections of the book read aloud

Videos
Watch informative video clips

Weblinks
Gain additional information for research

Try This!
Complete activities and hands-on experiments

Key Words
Study vocabulary, and complete a matching word activity

Quizzes
Test your knowledge

Slideshows
View images and captions

... and much, much more!

NATURAL WONDERS OF THE WORLD

NILE RIVER

Contents

The River of Life

The Nile River in Africa has supplied precious water to human civilizations for thousands of years. Water is an important issue in northern Africa since very dry land covers most of the region. In fact, the Nile River cuts right through the largest desert in the world, the Sahara. Along the banks of the Nile, however, life is possible.

The Nile brings drinking water to people. It allows farmers to raise crops. People fish in the Nile's waters. The river provides a transportation channel so people can travel on boats. Thousands of years ago, Ancient Egyptians used the same river for identical reasons. Not surprisingly, people often refer to the Nile as "the River of Life."

Dams on the Nile River help to provide people with both water and power. They also prevent flooding.

Reptiles such as the Nile crocodile live in and around the Nile River because of its plentiful water supply.

Nile River Facts

- The Nile River is 4,132 miles (6,650 kilometers) long. This makes it the longest river in the world.

- The Nile River is unusual because it begins in the south and flows north. Most rivers flow north to south.

- The largest city along the Nile is Cairo, Egypt. It has the second-largest population of any city in Africa, after Lagos, Nigeria.

- In 1902, the Aswan Dam was the first dam built on the Nile.

Mapping the Nile River

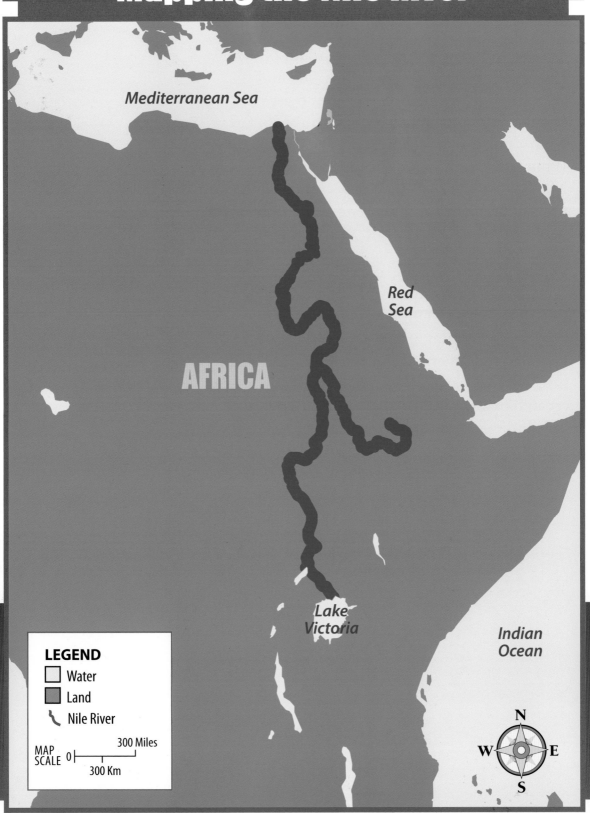

Mediterranean Sea

Red Sea

AFRICA

Lake Victoria

Indian Ocean

LEGEND
- Water
- Land
- Nile River

MAP SCALE

0   300 Miles

300 Km

N W E S

Where in the World?

The Nile River begins as two main branches in central Africa, the White Nile and the Blue Nile. These two branches twist and curve, and generally flow north to Khartoum, Sudan. There, the Blue and White Nile rivers meet, forming the main Nile River. The river then flows up through northeastern Africa until it empties into the Mediterranean Sea.

On its long and winding course, the Nile passes through different environments and various sites. There are swamplands and farmlands, large cities and tiny villages. Pyramids, temples, and other ancient treasures overlook the Nile riverbanks. There is even a huge lake created by humans. All of these and other fascinating sites await a Nile explorer.

The Blue Nile and White Nile were named for the color of the water in them. The Blue Nile is bright blue, and the While Nile is white-gray.

The Nile River makes its way over several waterfalls. In Uganda, water flows 141 feet (43 meters) down Murchison Falls.

Puzzler

The Nile River, including the Blue and White Nile, twists its way from central Africa up to the northern tip of the continent. In all, the river crosses the borders of 10 countries. **Can you identify the following countries through which the Nile passes? Match the countries listed below with their corresponding number.**

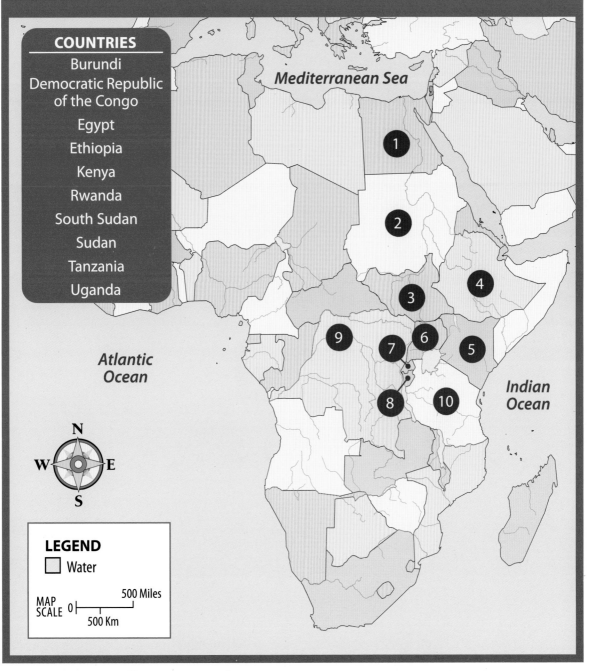

COUNTRIES
Burundi
Democratic Republic of the Congo
Egypt
Ethiopia
Kenya
Rwanda
South Sudan
Sudan
Tanzania
Uganda

Mediterranean Sea

Atlantic Ocean

Indian Ocean

LEGEND
☐ Water

MAP SCALE 0 |——|——| 500 Miles
            500 Km

ANSWERS: 1. Egypt **2.** Sudan **3.** Sudan **4.** Ethiopia **5.** Kenya **6.** Uganda **7.** Rwanda **8.** Burundi **9.** Democratic Republic of the Congo **10.** Tanzania

Nile River   7

A Trip Back in Time

Nearly 250 million years ago, Earth's continents split apart from a single, gigantic landmass. Africa then drifted to the place where it rests today. Although Africa stopped drifting, it has never stopped moving. **Geologists** believe that, for millions of years, a gradually growing **rift** has been pulling the continent in different directions. The rift is caused by shifting pressure from deep underground.

The rift has already created mountains and valleys on Africa's surface. In some of the valleys, bodies of water have formed. Many of the Nile's sources were formed by the rift, including its major source, Lake Victoria. If the rift continues to grow, geologists believe that larger bodies of water will form. Eventually, an entire ocean could divide the continent. It would take millions of years for this to happen, though.

Lake Victoria falls within the countries of Kenya, Uganda, and Tanzania. It is one of the 15 Great Lakes of Africa.

The Ethiopian Rift Valley stretches all across Ethiopia, from the Red Sea to the border with Kenya.

Parts of a River

Not every river is the same, but almost all have these main parts, which help to explain how a river works.

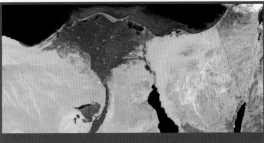

Mouth
The place where the river ends and travels to sea

Trunk
The main channel, or "trunk stream," of the river

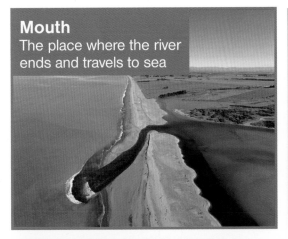

Delta
The land created by **sediment** the river leaves behind as it travels to sea

Tributaries
The rivers and streams that feed water into the main river

Basin
The surrounding land drained by the river and its tributaries

Headwaters
The beginning, main source of the river

Water at Work

Water is a necessary resource to every person on Earth, but water can be hard to obtain in the Nile region. Nile River communities are surrounded by desert. They would vanish if the Nile were to run dry.

Earth recycles its water. This means that today, people along the Nile might be using the same water that Ancient Egyptians did. The water cycle describes the way water moves above, on, and below ground. The cycle has four stages.

Evaporation
When water evaporates, it changes from a liquid to a gas, or vapor. Heat from the Sun speeds up evaporation.

Runoff
Runoff is precipitation that flows into rivers and streams. Runoff water flows above or below ground. Floods occur when too much runoff forces bodies of water to rise over their banks.

Storage
Water is stored in oceans, lakes, rivers, and underground. In cold climates, water is also stored in frozen glaciers and icecaps.

Precipitation
Water vapor collects in clouds. It then falls to the ground as precipitation, such as rain or snow. Every day, precipitation is falling somewhere in the world.

The Nile's Water

The Nile River is part of the water cycle. It is involved in evaporation, runoff, storage, and precipitation. Using the information provided about the water cycle stages, it is easy to understand how the Nile functions.

The Nile is a river, so it stores water. Water also evaporates from the Nile. In one part of the Blue Nile, the water flows into a massive swamp called the Sudd. In this shallow, hot area, water moves much more slowly than in other parts of the river. About half of the Sudd waters are lost to evaporation.

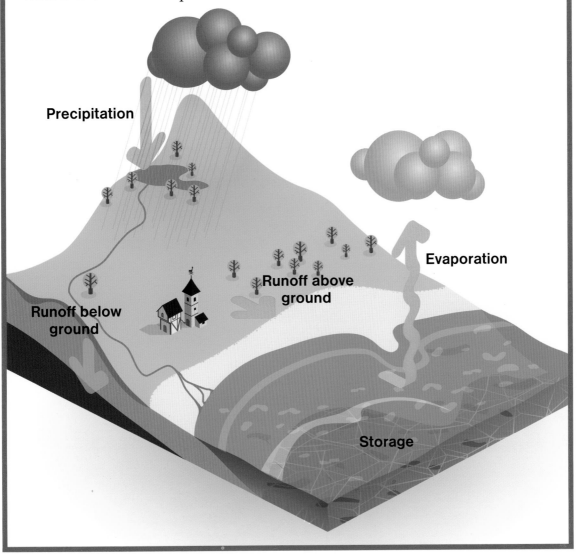

Precipitation

Evaporation

Runoff above ground

Runoff below ground

Storage

Life along the River

Hundreds of **species** of plants and animals make their homes in the Nile and along its banks. One of the most common plants found on the Nile shores is papyrus. This long reed has been used by people for thousands of years to make all sorts of objects, such as baskets, roofs for homes, and boats.

Giant Nile perch swim in the waters of the river. These fish grow to be 6 feet (1.8 m) long. Crocodiles and hippopotamuses also live in the water, coming ashore to bask in the sunlight. Bird life along the Nile is varied and vibrant. Beautiful flocks of white egrets hunt the shores for insects and frogs to eat. Swallows, ducks, warblers, and other bird types also live along the Nile.

Hippopotamuses spend up to 16 hours a day in the water. They are good swimmers and can hold their breath underwater for up to 5 minutes.

The hoopoe is a unique bird that lives near the Nile. It nests in holes that already exist in trees or cliffs.

Lake Nasser

In 1970, the Aswan High Dam was completed. The dam created a huge lake called Lake Nasser to hold floodwaters. Certain animals have benefited from the new lake, as they have an **ecosystem** in which they can thrive. Fish, birds, mammals, and reptiles now have a home where there was once only rock and sand.

The common spoonbill has the widest range of all spoonbills. It can be found in Europe, Japan, and northeast Africa.

Dorcas gazelles are well-suited to the deserts of northern Africa. They rarely need to drink water.

Egyptian geese are known for their distinctive calls. Males hiss, and females sound a loud, trumpet-like honk.

Pelicans are best-known for their deep throat pouch, which they use to catch fish.

The Nile monitor lizard is the largest lizard in Africa. It can grow to be 7 feet (2.1 m) long.

Early Explorers

The great civilizations of Ancient Egypt were built on the shores of the Nile about 5,000 years ago. Today, people are amazed by the huge pyramids and temples the Egyptians built without the aid of heavy machines. For centuries, Ancient Egyptians and many other civilizations were not able to solve one mystery of the Nile. They could not determine the source of the river.

Many explorers attempted to travel the entire course of the Nile to discover its source. It was not until recent centuries when a few determined explorers solved the puzzle, piece by piece. In 1770, Scottish explorer James Bruce found Lake Tana and the river now known as the Blue Nile while traveling overland in Africa. He sailed the river. When it joined with the main Nile, he knew he had discovered a Nile source, Lake Tana. Nearly a century later, in 1858, a British explorer named John Hanning Speke made another discovery. He was the first to learn that Lake Victoria is the source of the White Nile. Unfortunately, Europeans did not believe Speke's claim until other explorers proved him correct years later.

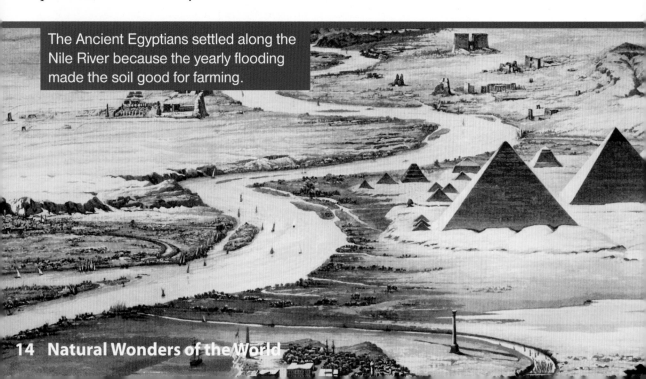

The Ancient Egyptians settled along the Nile River because the yearly flooding made the soil good for farming.

Biography

Dr. David Livingstone (1813–1873)
Sir Henry Morton Stanley (1841–1904)

In the mid-1800s, Africa was still a mysterious continent to Europeans. Dr. David Livingstone, a British explorer, did more than any other person to uncover Africa's mysteries. On his third and final African adventure, Livingstone's goal was to prove whether or not Lake Victoria was the source of the Nile.

Livingstone departed in 1866 and was not heard from for several years. In 1869, a United States newspaper sent another explorer, Henry Stanley, into Africa to find Livingstone. On November 10, 1871, Stanley found him in an African village surrounded by **indigenous** people.

Stanley and Livingstone continued exploring together briefly. Stanley left Africa to report Livingstone's story to the world. Dr. Livingstone became ill and died in Africa in 1873. Stanley, however, returned to Africa for years of further exploration. In 1875, he made a careful survey of Lake Victoria and finally proved that it was, indeed, the source of the Nile.

Stanley found Livingstone in the village of Ujiji, Tanzania.

Facts of Life

Dr. David Livingstone

- Born: March 19, 1813
- Hometown: Blantyre, Scotland
- Occupation: Doctor, missionary, explorer
- Died: May 1, 1873

Sir Henry Morton Stanley

- Born: January 28, 1841
- Hometown: Denbigh, Wales
- Occupation: Soldier, journalist, explorer
- Died: May 10, 1904

The Big Picture

Incredible rivers can be found all over the world. While some flow toward oceans, others empty into lakes. There are long and well-known rivers on every continent.

North America

Pacific Ocean

Atlantic Ocean

South America

Mississippi River
2,340 miles (3,766 km)
North America

Amazon River
4,000 miles (6,437 km)
South America

LEGEND
- ☐ Water
- ■ Land
- ☐ Antarctica
- ⌇ River

MAP SCALE 0   2,000 Miles
      2,000 Km

N W E S

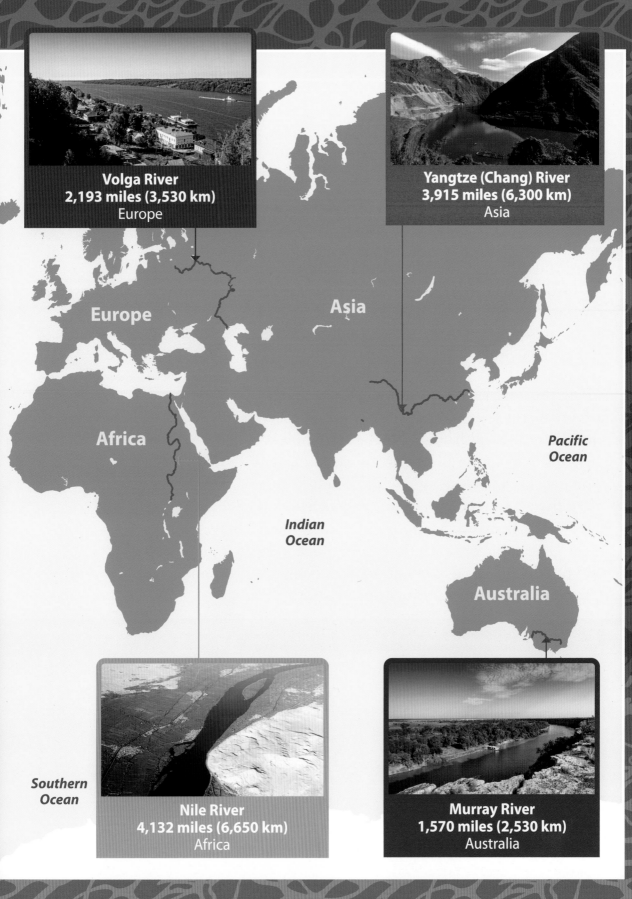

Volga River
2,193 miles (3,530 km)
Europe

Yangtze (Chang) River
3,915 miles (6,300 km)
Asia

Europe

Asia

Africa

Pacific
Ocean

Indian
Ocean

Australia

Southern
Ocean

Nile River
4,132 miles (6,650 km)
Africa

Murray River
1,570 miles (2,530 km)
Australia

People of the River

The Nile is no longer just the site of an ancient civilization. Today, the Nile River basin is home to about 257 million people. Cairo, Egypt, is a city bursting at its seams with almost 8 million people. The streets are busy with traffic, and tall, modern buildings fill the skyline. People work in office buildings, factories, universities, and other places. People from the very rich to the very poor live in this place, making Cairo a modern city of the world.

Along the Nile, however, not all communities are prosperous. For instance, Ethiopia is a world far different from Cairo. Most people near this part of the Blue Nile are rural farmers who never come close to city life. Their lives are difficult. In recent decades, **droughts** and civil war have led to **famine**. Millions of innocent people have died. Charitable organizations work hard to raise money and provide medical care and food to people in Ethiopia, Uganda, and other central African nations.

Droughts in Ethiopia make it difficult for farmers to grow crops and raise healthy livestock.

Cairo, Egypt, became a city more than 1,000 years ago.

Old and Modern

Imagine living in a place where there are reminders of ancient history just about everywhere. Every day along the Nile, residents live alongside examples of the distant past. The 3,000-year-old Luxor Temple is located in the middle of the modern city of Luxor. People can visit this amazing **artifact** in the course of running daily errands. In Cairo, ancient royal palaces have been turned into modern hotels.

Living in the cradle of ancient history has both good and bad elements. For instance, the tourists who visit these sites spend money that helps the area's economies. The cost of **preserving** these sites, however, is very high. A large portion of the money that tourists spend in the area does not actually help the people. Instead, much of the money is spent on maintaining the ancient artifacts.

Today, Luxor Temple is lit by modern electricity and surrounded by a city of more than 500,000 people.

Timeline

30 million years ago
The Nile River begins to form.

1700 AD
James Bruce reaches the source of the Blue Nile.

1858
John Hanning Speke finds that Lake Victoria is the source of the Nile.

30 million years ago	3000 BC	1500 AD	1840	1860	1880

3100 BC
Kingdoms along the Nile join, forming the Egyptian Empire.

1871
Sir Henry Morton Stanley and Dr. David Livingstone meet in Africa and begin exploring together.

1999
The Nile Basin Agreement is formed between the countries through which the Nile passes. This agreement attempts to undo the unfair 1959 treaty.

2012
Egypt opposes Ethiopia's proposed 6,000-megawatt hydroelectric dam on a Nile tributary.

1959
A treaty is signed between Egypt and Sudan, giving Egypt control of most of the Nile water. The treaty will harm other Nile nations in years to come.

1900   1920   1940   1960   1980   2000   2020

1902
The first Aswan Dam is completed. It is the first dam built on the Nile.

2019
More than 250 people volunteer to clean trash from the Nile River near Cairo.

Key Issue

Controlling the River

Since ancient times, people have attempted to control the Nile's floods and make better use of the Nile's water. Over the last century, humans have made major changes to the river. In 1970, the Aswan High Dam was completed. It ended the damaging floods that occurred along the Nile almost every year. The dam includes a power plant that provides electricity to most of Egypt. It also created the huge Lake Nasser **reservoir**.

In addition to blocking water, the dam stops most sediment from traveling up the Nile. This sediment contains important **nutrients** that help create the rich farmland that exists along the river. The entire Nile Delta is land created by thousands of years of sediment pouring from the Nile's mouth.

Today, very little sediment reaches the delta, so the quality of the soil suffers. Some farmers use chemicals to keep their soil healthy. Many scientists believe that foods grown with such chemicals are dangerous to eat. Scientists also believe that the chemicals wash back into the Nile, which can poison its water. So, for all the many benefits a dam can provide, there are quite a few drawbacks as well.

The Aswan High Dam feeds 12 power turbines and helps to meet Egypt's power demands.

Should humans build dams to control the Nile?

Yes	No
Dams create reservoirs that supply water to people who live nearby. They also run power plants.	Dams stop needed water from reaching places further along the river.
Dams control seasonal flooding that destroys people's homes along the river.	Annual flooding supplied the river's farms with nutrient-rich soil. Now, the farms do not receive those nutrients. Farmers use chemicals instead.
Dams make it easier to travel by boat on the river by controlling the flow of water.	Dams force people from their homes and destroy historical sites by creating new reservoirs.

The soil in the Nile Delta is becoming saltier, which makes it more difficult for crops to grow.

Natural Attractions

There are many things to see and do on a trip to the Nile River. People tour the river on cruise ships or on traditional boats called *feluccas*. In some Nile cities, visitors can step off the boats and walk directly to museums, restaurants, or shopping districts.

Visitors also travel the Nile River to see the river's more natural wonders. The spectacular Tisisat Falls on the Blue Nile draws visitors who travel to Ethiopia. Another popular site is Lake Victoria, the headwaters of the Nile. It is the second-largest freshwater lake in the world. On its islands and shores, visitors can camp, fish, and observe a wondrous array of wildlife.

Feluccas are a type of wooden sailboat.

Tisisat Falls is also called "The Nile That Smokes" because of the mist this strong waterfall creates.

Ancient Fruit

From thousands of years ago to today, dates have been one of the favorite foods of Egypt. **Archaeologists** exploring ancient pyramids have found dates placed inside tombs. Presumably, this was so the dead person sealed in the tomb would have something to eat in the afterlife.

Dates are the fruit of the date palm tree. After picking the fruit, farmers leave dates in the sunlight to dry. They become a sweet, chewy food similar to raisins. Date palms grow well in desert conditions, so dates are a **staple food** in certain parts of northern Africa.

The countries that produce the most dates each year are all in the Middle East. The top producers are Egypt, Iran, and Saudi Arabia.

River Stories

Ancient Egyptians believed in many gods and goddesses who ruled different parts of nature. The Nile River was so important that the Egyptians believed it was controlled by a god named Osiris. According to Egyptian mythology, Osiris was a ruler of Egypt who was murdered by his jealous brother, Seth. Osiris's body was cut up, placed in a coffin, and sent floating down the Nile. He eventually came back to life as a god.

Cleopatra became the queen of Egypt in 51 BC.

The Nile has also inspired more recent authors to write novels, poems, and stories about the river. In the early 1600s, British playwright William Shakespeare wrote a well-known play called *Antony and Cleopatra*. It is based on the real-life story of Cleopatra, an Ancient Egyptian ruler who was nicknamed "the Queen of the Nile." In 1937, author Agatha Christie wrote one of her best-known mystery novels, *Death on the Nile*, about murder and suspicion aboard a Nile River cruise.

Osiris is most often shown with either green or black skin, which represents rebirth and the soil of the land along the Nile.

Ramses II

One of the great stories of the Bible is linked to a leader from Egypt's past. Ramses II was pharaoh of Egypt from 1279 to 1213 BC. He was well known for building magnificent temples along the Nile River.

Today, however, people may know Ramses II more for his role in the biblical story of Moses. According to the Bible, Ramses II ruled over Jewish slaves in Egypt and refused to release them to freedom. The Jewish people's leader, Moses, engaged Ramses II in a battle of wills. Eventually, Ramses II freed Moses's people. Today, Jewish people celebrate this story during the Passover holiday.

Abu Simbel is one of the two large temples that were built during Ramses II's reign.

What Have You Learned?

True or False?

Decide whether the following statements are true or false.
If the statement is false, make it true.

1. Papyrus grows along the Nile River.

2. Ramses II was a slave in Egypt.

3. The source of the Nile River is unknown.

4. Dr. David Livingstone explored Africa several times.

5. Rivers can be found on every continent.

6. The water cycle does not need the Sun.

Short Answer

Answer the following questions using information from the book.

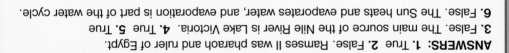

1. Is the mouth of the Nile at its beginning or its end?

2. What fruit grows along the Nile?

3. Who wrote *Antony and Cleopatra*?

4. When was the Aswan High Dam completed?

5. Through how many different countries does the Nile River pass?

Multiple Choice

Choose the best answer for the following questions.

1. People along the Nile make paper from:

    a. palm tree bark
    b. sediment
    c. papyrus
    d. stone

2. Which of the following statements is incorrect?

    a. The Nile is the longest river in the world.
    b. Africa might split apart several million
       years from now.
    c. Lake Nasser existed during the time
       of Ancient Egypt.
    d. Cairo is the largest city along the Nile.

3. Where do the White Nile and Blue Nile meet?

    a. Khartoum
    b. Cairo
    c. Luxor
    d. Kampala

4. Which of these countries does not have
part of the Nile within its borders?

    a. Rwanda
    b. Egypt
    c. South Sudan
    d. Zimbabwe

ANSWERS: 1. c 2. c 3. a 4. d

Activity

Build a Waterwheel

Water is a very powerful resource. Countries along the Nile River rely on its water to **irrigate** crops and to provide electricity. The development of dams along the river demonstrate the importance of this resource to the area's economy. You can learn more about the power of water by building a waterwheel.

Materials

- A foam ball
- A long skewer or stick about twice the length of the ball
- A sink or large bowl
- A large cup
- Plastic spoons
- Water

Instructions

1. Poke the skewer through the center of the ball.

2. Wiggle the skewer until the ball easily spins around it.

3. Place the plastic spoons evenly in a row around the ball. Stick the handles into the ball, and make sure the scoops all face up.

4. Hold the ball by the skewer over the sink.

5. Fill the cup with water. Raise the cup of water as high as you can. Pour the water over your waterwheel. What happens? Try pouring the water from higher and lower heights. Does the height change how the waterwheel spins? If so, why do you think this happens?

Key Words

archaeologists: scientists who study past people and cultures

artifact: an object made by humans; a historical object in a museum

droughts: long periods of dry weather

ecosystem: a group of living plants, animals, and their environment, all of which act as a community

famine: starvation of large numbers of people

geologists: scientists who study rocks, soils, and minerals

indigenous: native to a certain place, having been born in a place

irrigate: to supply with water

nutrients: any substance that provides nourishment

preserving: saving for the future; shielding from destruction

reservoir: a holding area to store water

rift: a long, narrow crack; a place where land is pulling apart

sediment: material deposited by water, wind, or glaciers

species: a specific group of plant or animal that shares characteristics

staple food: a food that is eaten regularly and is kept in large amounts

Index

Get the best of both worlds.

AV2 bridges the gap between print and digital.

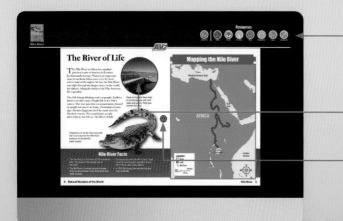

The expandable resources toolbar enables quick access to content including **videos**, **audio**, **activities**, **weblinks**, **slideshows**, **quizzes**, and **key words**.

Animated videos make static images come alive.

Resource icons on each page help readers to further **explore key concepts**.

Published by AV2
350 5th Avenue, 59th Floor
New York, NY 10118
Website: www.av2books.com

Library of Congress Control Number: 2019954626

ISBN 978-1-7911-2067-2 (hardcover)
ISBN 978-1-7911-2068-9 (softcover)
ISBN 978-1-7911-2069-6 (multi-user eBook)
ISBN 978-1-7911-2070-2 (single-user eBook)

Printed in Guangzhou, China
1 2 3 4 5 6 7 8 9 24 23 22 21 20

022020
101319

Project Coordinator Heather Kissock
Designers Ana Maria Vidal, Tammy West, and Terry Paulhus

Every reasonable effort has been made to trace ownership and to obtain permission to reprint copyright material. The publishers would be pleased to have any errors or omissions brought to their attention so that they may be corrected in subsequent printings.

Photo Credits
AV2 acknowledges Getty Images, Alamy, iStock, Shutterstock, and Newscom as its primary photo suppliers for this title.